This is a fictionalised biography describing some of the key moments (so far!) in the career of Jadon Sancho.

Some of the events described in this book are based upon the author's imagination and are probably not entirely accurate representations of what actually happened.

Tales from the Pitch
Jadon Sancho
by Harry Coninx

Published by Raven Books
An imprint of Ransom Publishing Ltd.
Unit 7, Brocklands Farm, West Meon, Hampshire GU32 1JN, UK
www.ransom.co.uk

ISBN   978 178591 980 0
First published in 2021
Reprinted 2021

Copyright © 2021 Ransom Publishing Ltd.
Text copyright © 2021 Ransom Publishing Ltd.
Cover illustration by Ben Farr © 2021 Ben Farr

A CIP catalogue record of this book is available from the British Library.

All rights reserved. No part of this publication may be reproduced, stored in a retrieval system, or transmitted, in any form or by any means, electronic, mechanical, photocopying, recording or otherwise, without the prior permission of the publishers.

The rights of Harry Coninx to be identified as the author and of Ben Farr to be identified as the illustrator of this Work have been asserted by them in accordance with sections 77 and 78 of the Copyright, Design and Patents Act 1988.

TALES FROM THE PITCH

JADON SANCHO

HARRY CONINX

For Masood, the Reiss Nelson to my Jadon Sancho

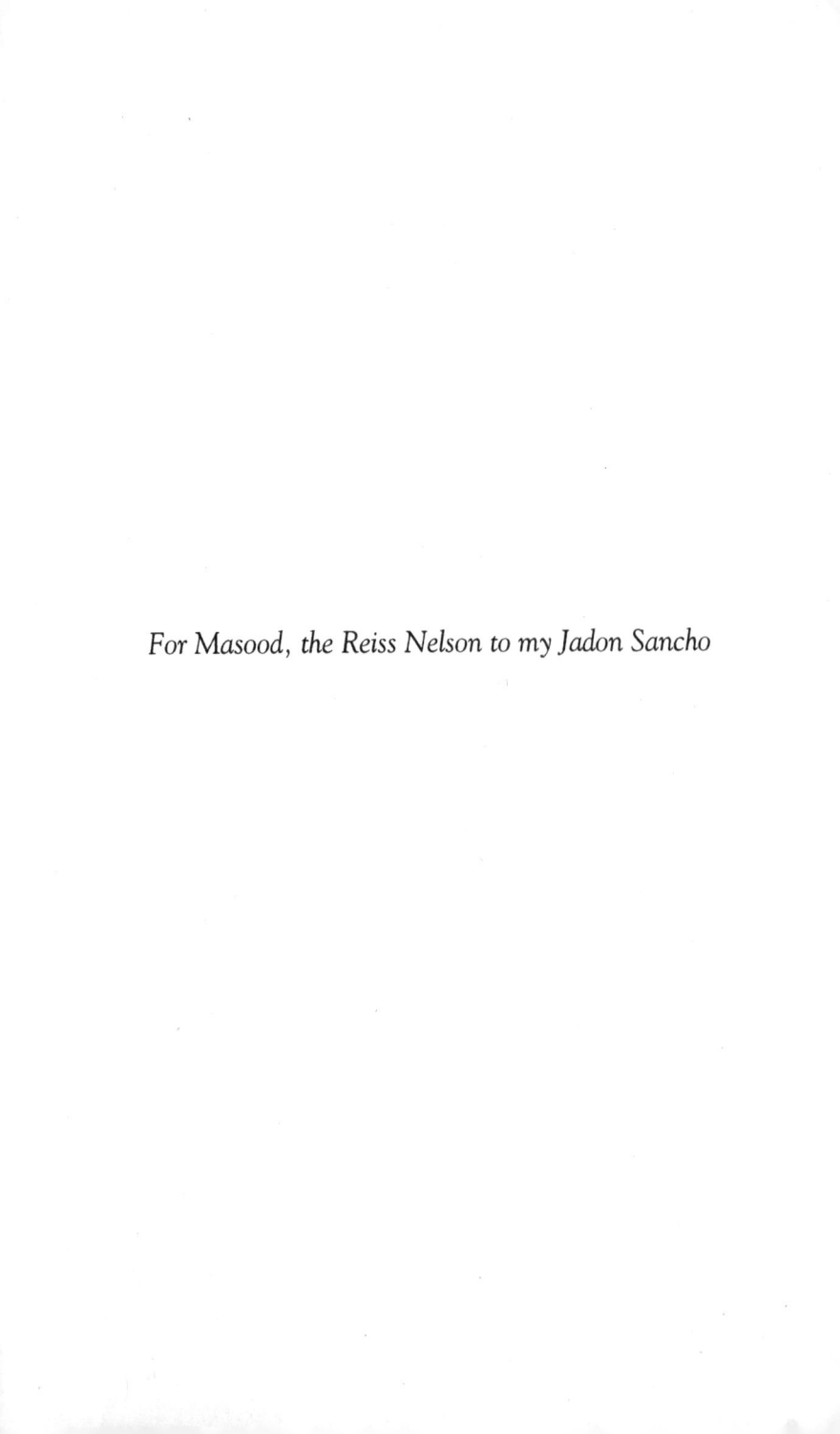

CONTENTS

		Page
1	The Jadon Sancho Show	7
2	Street Football	15
3	*That* Good	22
4	The Hornets	27
5	Due North	35
6	A City Player	40
7	Pepped	44
8	Friend and Foe	50
9	Playing the Game	55
10	A New Path	63
11	Chile in the Heat	68
12	Debut	74
13	Back in the Game	78
14	On the Bench	87
15	"It's Gareth"	92
16	A Starter for Two	95
17	Doubts	99
18	Making It Happen	108
19	Hat-Trick	114

I
THE JADON SANCHO SHOW

August 2019, Signal Iduna Park, Dortmund, Germany
Borussia Dortmund v Bayern Munich

The crowd was a sea of yellow and black, and a deafening wall of noise rose up from every corner of the stadium.

Jadon had been at Dortmund for over two years now, but he still struggled to get used to the atmosphere. The game hadn't even begun, but the noise was already louder than any stadium he'd played in.

He was supposed to be warming up for the game, but instead he was trading skills with Mario Götze. He flicked the ball up, juggling it a couple of times before volleying it back to Mario.

Mario controlled the ball with his chest, then fired it back at Jadon.

"Mario! Jadon!" The shout came from Dortmund captain Marco Reus.

Jadon stopped the ball dead on the ground, irritated by his captain's interruption.

"We need to be doing proper warm-ups," said Reus. "It's the first game of the season and we're rusty enough as it is."

"Does it look like I need to warm up?" Jadon laughed, sprinting towards his captain and flicking the ball between his legs.

Reus shook his head in despair and looked across to the Dortmund manager, who'd obviously asked his captain to get the team in line.

"Fine, whatever," Reus muttered, turning back to his own running drills and leaving Jadon to sort out his own warm-up.

Jadon had always found the running drills dull. He didn't need to practise this stuff – he needed to be on the pitch, playing against another team.

It didn't matter if it was on a concrete playground in south London or in front of 80,000 people at the Signal Iduna Park. As soon as the game got going, so did Jadon.

And today's game was huge – the German Super Cup was at stake.

All that stood in their way was Bayern Munich, the team that had done the double last season, winning the German Cup and the Bundesliga, thanks to players like Lewandowski, Müller and Neuer.

The warm-ups over, the players were soon back in the dressing room, listening carefully to their manager's team talk.

"We know how good Bayern are," said Lucien Favre, looking serious, "and we know what qualities they have. But we want to win the league this year, right boys?"

"If we win tonight, we send out a big message, lads," Marco Reus stepped in, taking over from the gaffer.

"We're telling the world that we're ready to take the title back from Bayern."

"So let's go out there and do it!" Axel Witsel roared.

Jadon joined in their enthusiasm. If you couldn't get yourself up for *this* game, then you didn't belong on a football pitch.

Both teams were desperate to win and the game was played at a high pace. Super Cup or not, any game between Bayern and Dortmund was going to be massive.

Paco Alcácer saw a couple of shots skid past the post, and at the other end Dortmund keeper Marwin Hitz was forced into a number of crucial saves.

At half-time the game was still deadlocked at 0-0.

"We've been the better team, lads," Reus said, clapping his hands as they re-entered the tunnel at half-time. "We get the first goal, I make us favourites."

Jadon had struggled with stiff legs in the first half, and for the first time in his life he wondered if Marco Reus had been right about warm-ups.

"Keep going out there, Jadon," Reus said, leaning over to him. "They're terrified of your pace – that's why they've got two guys on you."

"Yeah, I know," Jadon nodded.

"But if you keep working, eventually they'll tire and then you'll get the space you need."

Barely a minute into the second half, Jadon got the space he'd been desperate for. He skipped past Jérôme Boateng and found his way into the box. With a crowd of Bayern players around him, he stabbed the ball between the legs of Corentin Tolisso, towards Paco Alcácer.

Alcácer struck the ball first time from the edge of the box, and he watched it bounce past Neuer and into the Bayern goal.

"You just can't resist a nutmeg, can you?" Reus said, as they celebrated the opener.

"Makes the goal a hundred times better, doesn't it?" Jadon replied with a grin.

Despite the goal, they knew that the game was far from won. Bayern weren't a team to let a game get away from them easily, and they started getting all the possession, with Dortmund defending desperately in front of their own goal.

"Let's keep our focus, lads!" Ömer Toprak shouted from the back. "We can't let this get away from us now."

With twenty minutes left, Jadon found some space down the right-hand side. He sprinted clear, away from the chasing defenders, and burst forward into the box.

The Bayern keeper Manuel Neuer came out quickly, trying to close down the angle between Jadon and the goal.

Neuer made himself big, but Jadon had been working on his finishing. He did what he always did – and slipped it between the keeper's legs.

As the ball rolled into the net, Jadon was already sprinting towards the corner flag, leaping into the air and punching the sky.

"Another nutmeg, huh?" Marco Reus said drily, a big smile on his face.

"I'm telling you, it makes the goal a lot better," Jadon insisted.

The game was pretty much done from that point. First game of the season, both teams were still struggling for fitness, and Bayern didn't have the energy to get the game back.

With ten minutes remaining, the substitute's board went up with Jadon's famous number 7 on it.

As Jadon went off, there was a standing ovation from every corner of the ground. He was voted Man of the Match and he'd won the trophy but – most important – he'd helped his team beat Bayern Munich.

"It's been the Jadon Sancho show out there today!" Lucien Favre exclaimed, as Jadon stumbled towards the bench. "I brought you off because I wanted you to hear the fans. Just listen! You're a Dortmund legend!"

Minutes later, the game was over. Dortmund had won the first trophy of the season and they'd beaten their famous rivals, Bayern Munich. It was Jadon's first trophy as a professional.

"This is amazing, man," he gasped, as they collected their medals.

"This isn't even a *proper* one," Marco Reus grinned. "Wait 'til we win the cup or the league. And we will, if we keep playing like we did today – or rather, if YOU keep playing anything like *you* did today."

Moments later, Reus held the trophy aloft. Jadon looked at it, savouring the moment. His career was still in its early stages, but he knew one thing already.

This would not be the last trophy he would win.

2
STREET FOOTBALL

March 2008, Frederick's adventure playground
South London, England

"Jadon! Come on! Be on our team!" one of the boys shouted, over the noise of the London traffic.

Jadon smiled and kicked the tin can he'd been doing keepy-uppies with to the side of the cage. At last, there were enough boys at the park to get a match going.

It was a crowded concrete pitch and, being only eight, Jadon was one of the youngest there.

He had to move fast, or he'd get knocked over.

He'd been playing like this since he was five years old and it was how he'd got to be so good.

Street football was nothing like football on TV, or when he'd been training at Watford's development academy. Here there were no rules, no offside and no referees. If you got fouled, you just had to play on.

With his first touch, he flicked the ball round one player and was already moving past him, getting the ball on to the other side.

He barely had time to breathe before the next player was closing him down. Jadon tapped the ball against the side of the cage, bouncing it round the other player.

Then he faced the next defender and quickly saw a chance to use a trick he'd been working on ever since he'd seen Ronaldinho do it – the flip flap.

Jadon flicked the ball between the outside and inside of his boot, then tapped it between the legs of the defender.

"Nuts!" someone roared and a few chuckles went up, everyone revelling in the older boy's embarrassment.

But Jadon was already past the player and now he

had his sights on scoring. He could see it all in his mind's eye, just as Ronaldinho had done against Real Madrid all those years ago.

He lashed his foot through the ball and it sailed into the top corner of the 'goal'.

He wheeled round, triumphantly waving his arms in the air.

"I told you he'd be able to do that trick in an actual game," one of the boys boasted.

"This kid can play!" said another.

But a shout from the keeper wiped the smiles off their faces.

"No goal!"

"What are you talking about?" Jadon yelled, over the protests from the rest of his team. "That was top corner."

"Nah, it was over the bar," the keeper bellowed, tapping where the ball had supposedly landed, then staring Jadon down.

This was the trouble with playing without real goalposts, without anything to show whether a shot was on target or not.

Jadon hadn't seen where the ball had gone, but he didn't bother arguing. He had an instinct for how to deal with things, and arguing with this guy would get him nowhere. Better to play on and score again.

So that's exactly what he did.

Then he scored again, his third of the game.

And he was just about to score a fourth, going for another nutmeg, when he was clattered to the floor by someone behind him.

He went flying on to the rough concrete, putting his hands out to break his fall. He felt the skin break.

He looked up to see the older boy he'd nutmegged earlier, before his first – disallowed – goal.

"You had that coming, bro," the boy smirked, before flicking the ball away from Jadon and kicking it down the pitch.

Jadon grimaced and picked himself up, wiping his hands on his shorts and wincing at the sting of his grazed hands.

That was the thing about trying new skills on the bigger boys – they didn't like being shown up and often found ways to get back at you.

This is how it was with street football.

"That's why we play on grass, Jadon."

It was a man's voice, and Jadon turned to see Norman, the guy who ran the youth football club that Jadon played for at weekends.

"Hurts just as much on grass when someone kicks you in the ankle," Jadon fired back with a grin. "Still worth it, though."

"I'm not sure I agree," said a second man, stepping out of the shadows.

Jadon recognised him – it was Dave Godley, a coach from Watford. He'd been working with Jadon over the past few years and had been keeping a close eye on him recently. Jadon had just had his eighth birthday, which meant that he could now sign a schoolboy contract with the club. For Jadon, that was huge.

"Where else am I supposed to practice?" Jadon asked, looking at Dave.

"At home," Dave replied, "wrapped up in cotton wool." He chuckled at his own joke, then looked serious. "You're sure you can't sign a contract tomorrow, Jadon?" he asked.

So Dave wasn't here by accident. He'd come to the park today because he was worried that word might get out about Jadon. He couldn't risk other clubs trying to snatch him from Watford.

"No, I need my family with me," said Jadon. "It has to be Saturday, after the tournament."

"OK," Dave said, holding his hands up. "But just promise me you won't talk to anyone else. Watford is where you belong."

"Don't worry, Dave. I'm going to sign."

"And you're sure about playing in this tournament?" Dave asked, noticing a look of disapproval from Norman, who needed Jadon in his team to win the tournament.

"Of course!" Jadon almost shouted.

"That's my boy," Norman said with a grin. "You wouldn't miss a tournament like this for the world, would you? Plus, Reiss is playing."

Jadon smiled at the mention of his best friend, Reiss Nelson. Reiss was a year older than Jadon and was the only player anywhere near as good as him.

They'd met playing street football and Jadon liked

the way the rivalry between them pushed him on. And there was nothing better than when they played on the same team and absolutely destroyed the opposition.

"OK, Jadon," Dave said reluctantly, "but please, *please*, try not to get injured."

Jadon nodded, but a moment later he was back in the game, right in the thick of the action, being sent flying to floor by the latest challenge.

Dave looked at Norman, sighed and shook his head.

3
THAT GOOD

March 2008, sports ground, Kennington, South London, England

Saturday came around faster than Jadon had expected.

As he and his dad made their way into the ground, he was surprised to be feeling some nerves. He knew it wasn't because of the football – it was because of the Watford contract waiting for him after the match.

If Jadon signed he'd be committing his future to the club. He wouldn't be able to play street football with the other lads whenever he wanted, and he'd have to train properly every week.

"Thinking about the contract?" asked his dad, Sean. He could obviously sense Jadon's tension.

Jadon nodded and looked at his dad. "Do you think signing with them is the right thing to do?"

His dad put his arm around Jadon's shoulder. He was proud of Jadon as a footballer, but even more proud of the fact that, even at such a young age, his son had a good head on his shoulders.

"It's your life, Jadon," he said, "and I know you've got your dad's street smarts. You know deep down what the right thing to do is."

Jadon breathed in the cold spring air and thought about his options.

It was obvious that street football would soon become a thing of the past for him. After all the things Dave had said, he'd be daft to think otherwise.

But it was a four-hour commute from his parents' home in South London to Watford, on the outskirts of North London. That would be tough.

"I wish there was a big team here in Kennington that

me and Reiss could play for," he muttered under his breath. "Then we'd never have to move."

His dad laughed. "We've talked a lot about the sacrifices you're going to have to make to become the footballer you want to be, Jadon. You know what those sacrifices are. But you also know that I'll be with you all the way, if you think it's worth it."

"It's worth it," Jadon said resolutely.

He knew that this was the way ahead for him. "I want to sign for Watford's Academy. It'll be good for my football."

And with that he let the ball he'd been holding drop to his feet. His dad spun round to face him in a defensive position and Jadon ran at him, pretending to go one way but instead going the other.

It was as if the ball was glued to his feet and, even though his dad stuck out a leg, Jadon was already over it and away with the ball.

A shout came from across the pitch.

"Hey, Jadon! Why don't you pick on someone your own size?"

Jadon looked up to see Reiss smiling wickedly.

Jadon and Reiss were soon pinging the ball back and forth between them, seeing who had the better skills and who could do the crazier things with the ball.

Then Norman appeared and dragged them both off to join the rest of the team. "Save it for the games, lads," he laughed. "Don't waste it all out here."

The matches that day came thick and fast. Jadon was having the time of his life, nipping the ball off the toes of the opposition, playing quick one-twos with Reiss that no one could intercept, and beating defenders every time.

Norman's cheers were the loudest, but there were also shouts of appreciation from the groups of parents who were watching.

The tournament was over not long after it had begun. Jadon's team had ultimately been knocked out before the final, but they'd been playing at a level far above their age group, so Jadon wasn't too disappointed.

Jadon normally stuck around to have another kickabout with Reiss after the games, but this time they were interrupted by Jadon's dad.

"Nice work today, boys, but there's no time for a kickabout."

Jadon looked up, confused.

"Dave's here in his car," his dad explained. "He's worried that someone's going to try to nab you at the tournament, so he's giving us a lift to Watford now."

"He thinks other clubs are here?" Jadon scoffed. "There's only like ten people here! He's seriously paranoid."

His dad laughed, steering his son toward the car.

"Jadon, believe me. You're *that* good," was all he said.

4
THE HORNETS

April 2014, Harefield Academy, Watford, England

As Jadon got on the Watford bus, he saw plenty of nervous faces staring at him.

His fellow U15 team-mates might be feeling the pressure, but Jadon wasn't nervous at all. In fact he was happy – happy to be on his way to play another match and happy that he'd signed for this club.

It had been worth it, just as he'd expected.

But it hadn't been easy. The sacrifices his dad had warned him about had been hard.

The commute from his home to Watford had turned out to be too much for Jadon, so he'd had to move away from home at just 11 years old.

Now he was away from his family and his friends, boarding at the school in Watford that partnered with the club.

Missing his home and his friends was tough, and sometimes it made him play up in his school lessons at Harefield Academy.

Gradually, though, he settled into a regular routine. Morning classes were interrupted for football practice, but then he'd be back at school for afternoon lessons when the other kids went home, making up for lost lesson time, before training began again.

His mind was nearly always on football and he took every opportunity he could to play or to watch it. Sometimes he even got told off in ICT for watching Ronaldinho's best performances on YouTube.

It was relentless, but Jadon loved it. And his football was going from strength to strength. It was obvious from the first day that he was on another level, playing with flair and imagination, but with an edge too. There was still a bit of street football in him that training hadn't managed to eliminate completely.

His ability to run at people, to nutmeg, to drop his shoulder – he'd learnt all that on the streets.

But now he was combining it with what he was learning at Watford. Fitness, game management, positional play, discipline – Jadon took it all in.

He still got the chance to play on the streets when he went home. He'd often play with Reiss, who'd also been snapped up – by the very team that Watford were playing today. Arsenal.

That was why the rest of the U15s were sitting on the bus looking so worried.

As the boys settled on the bus, Dave gave them a pep talk.

"Right, lads!" he bellowed, silencing any conversations. "It's a big one tonight. We all know who Arsenal are and what they're capable of. But remember, when you get out on that pitch, it's just 11 red shirts versus 11 yellow shirts. Anything can happen. It's what we make it."

There were mutterings from the back of the bus. All the boys knew that those 11 red shirts would be worn by some of the best players in their age group.

What chance did they have?

"Hey! None of that," said Dave, before clapping eyes on Jadon. "Look, Jadon's not worried, are you Jadon?"

"*They're* the ones in trouble – they're playing against me," Jadon replied, with a directness and self-belief that quietened the nervous whispers on the bus.

As the bus pulled away, Jadon noticed that Dave was looking at him. Dave had worked so hard to get him here, and Jadon owed him for the faith he'd shown in him.

Just last week he and Dave had been sitting on the training ground talking to one of the other Watford youth coaches, Louis Lancaster, about Jadon's future.

"What's the dream?" Louis had asked him.

"Playing for one of Europe's top clubs and representing England," Jadon had replied without a moment's hesitation.

At Arsenal's ground, the boys piled out of the bus, changed and were straight into warm-ups. Jadon couldn't avoid looking to see if Reiss was in the opposition ranks, even though he knew he'd been moved up an age group.

"Jadon!" Dave shouted. "Come here!"

Jadon jogged over, not quite sure what the manager wanted.

"You inspired the boys on the bus, you know."

"Good," Jadon said.

The look on Dave's face was strange, as if there was something he didn't want to say.

"Look, I'm going to play you as a striker today," Dave said, "down the middle, like a standard number 9."

"What?" Jadon exclaimed. "But why? I'll never get the ball up there. I won't be in the game!"

"That's kind of the point," Dave continued, looking at the floor. "I don't want the scouts getting in your head. I don't want you impressing them too much."

In that moment Jadon felt all his energy, all his grit and his self-belief drop away.

Was he understanding this right? They were going to play him out of position, just so that another club wouldn't see him play well.

What was the point in that? That wasn't fair on his team-mates and it wasn't fair on him.

It was wrong.

"I know, I know, it's not right," said Dave quickly, reading the expression on Jadon's face and looking a little ashamed. "But see it as an opportunity to prove yourself in some different positions. You never know, you might even get a goal or two."

"OK, boss," Jadon sighed grudgingly. Then he trudged across the pitch, still feeling shocked and deflated.

As the kick-off approached, Jadon's mood changed to defiance.

They could try and play him out of position all they wanted, but he was still going to impress. He was going to drop deep and grab the ball anyway. He was going to do as many tricks and flicks as he could, and he was going to score the best goals he'd ever scored.

If this was the game they wanted to play – then game on!

By the time the match kicked off, he was more fired up about a single game than he'd ever been before in his life.

Arsenal had plenty of good players and Watford struggled to get much of the ball, just as they'd expected. But after about 10 minutes, Jadon got his first sniff. He dropped into midfield and picked up the ball. He spun one player and started sprinting at the centre-backs.

"Jadon! Out wide!"

He heard the shout from a team-mate, but Jadon only had one thing in his mind.

He pretended to shoot, the defender diving in front of him, but he kept the ball and pressed on. He dummied again, setting another defender down on the floor, and suddenly he was in the box.

He pulled back his left foot and rifled the ball into the bottom corner.

GOAL!

"How about that?" he roared, looking up at the sky. He was so pumped up about this game now that it wasn't about celebrating any more.

It was about proving a point.

He got a couple more chances, and each time he managed to skip past the Arsenal defenders, who just weren't a match for him.

His passing was also at its very best. Every time he picked the ball up, he'd ping it across the pitch, placing it precisely at the feet of one of his team-mates.

At the full-time whistle, Jason looked across at Dave. The boss was smiling at the incredible display of football he'd just witnessed, but it was a pained smile.

It was the smile of a man who knew that his team wouldn't be keeping this young player for very long.

5
DUE NORTH

March 2015, Watford training ground, Watford, England

Jadon looked down at the shiny new pair of boots in his hand, tracing the pattern of the design with his finger. His Watford team-mates stood around him.

"They're even better than the ones you got sent last week!" one of them exclaimed.

"Who are these ones from, Jadon?" another asked, grabbing the note that came with them.

Jadon shrugged, turning the boots over to examine the clean new studs.

Despite Dave's best efforts, word was out about Watford's wonder kid and for a while clubs and agents from around the country had been trying to turn Jadon's head.

Jadon wondered if some boys genuinely did change clubs over a new pair of boots. It was flattering, of course, but it wasn't going to work with him.

In any event, none of it mattered, because just that morning he'd had the confirmation that new contracts had been drawn up for him to join another club – the kind of club he'd once told the coaches he'd be playing for one day.

Man City.

His dad had always insisted that Jadon himself knew what was best for him, so he'd just been waiting on his son's decision.

If Jadon said yes, then they'd both make the move up north together, just as his dad had promised all those years ago.

Jadon knew that he was ready for the challenge,

ready to be pushed to become the best he could be. He needed to be tested by the incredible young players from around the world that City had assembled in their team.

Leaving London didn't faze him either. He knew he could cope. He'd done it before when he'd moved to Watford, and this time he'd even have his dad with him.

There was just one thing, lodged in the back of his mind, that he knew he'd have to think about very carefully.

His phone buzzed in his pocket and Jadon knew exactly who it was.

"MAN CITY!" Reiss shouted down the phone.

"I know," Jadon grinned, wandering out of the changing rooms and away from the boys, who were still admiring his new boots.

"Us London boys don't really go north, though," Reiss said, jokingly.

"How about Sterling?" Jadon replied.

"You're telling me that you're the new Sterling?" Reiss said, now laughing wildly.

Jadon waited for him to stop laughing, before sharing what was on his mind.

This was serious, and Jadon needed Reiss to know that.

"Reiss, how's it going at Arsenal, with all those big names?"

There was a pause before Reiss answered.

"Not too bad. There *is* pressure. You're fighting every day for the chance to prove yourself and, yeah, that's tough. But I think that makes me better ... more likely to get those chances, even if there aren't very many of them."

Jadon pressed the phone to his ear, listening to his friend's words carefully.

"Just like how I make you better when we kick about at the weekend, you know?" added Reiss.

It was Jadon's turn to laugh. Suddenly he felt more relaxed.

Listening to Reiss, he now knew he'd made his decision.

He could cope with the pressure and he had the grit to fight for his place.

He was going to Manchester.

6
A CITY PLAYER

March 2016, Manchester City Football Academy
Manchester, England

The first year at Manchester City had been an eye-opening experience for Jadon.

It had also been an exhausting one. For the first three months he hadn't played a game for any of the Academy sides, as they tried to get him up to speed with how Man City played.

It was a lot harder than at Watford, and there was a

real focus on holding on to the ball, passing and crossing. They weren't as keen on dribbling or long-range shooting.

But the coaches at the Academy clearly appreciated Jadon's abilities and were focused totally on helping him become the best player he could be.

Today's training session was no exception and Jadon heard the U18s manager, Jason Wilcox, shouting his name, sounding slightly exasperated at him for once more trying a nutmeg.

"Jadon!"

The manager gestured to the other side of the pitch, where Brahim Díaz had been waiting patiently for a pass that had never arrived.

"Sometimes it's the right moment for a nutmeg, and sometimes it's the right moment for a pass. City players can do both, you know!"

Jadon nodded, determination showing on his face. He wanted to learn and to improve, but he also wanted to be himself. He wanted to make the best use of the skills he already had.

"Same with your dribbling," Jason went on. "It's some

of the best I've seen from a player your age, but sometimes the best thing to do is to beat one man, then pass the ball. Don't take on too much – we're a team, and there are ten other players around you."

Within a few minutes Jadon had put the advice into practice, skipping past the challenge of a defender before sliding the ball to a striker, who slashed it past the post.

The coach's praise was music to Jadon's ears and he walked into the dressing room satisfied with another day's progress.

"Will we be seeing you on Saturday night, Jadon?" one of his teammates asked him, as they did most Fridays.

Jadon shook his head and gave his usual reply to the boys whenever they invited him out.

"No, I'm really sorry. I'm going back to London."

"One day we'll have to come down with you, Jadon, see one of these South London parties for ourselves."

"Parties?" Jadon asked, a look of surprise on his face. "I don't go to parties."

He looked at the blank faces around him and

shrugged. "I hang out with my friend, Reiss. We kick a ball around."

The boys started laughing.

"So let me get this right ... to relax, after playing football all week, you ... play *more* football?"

Jadon laughed too. He could see how it might seem odd to his team-mates, but for him it was simple – the more football he played, the better he would be.

"I want to play for England," Jadon said simply. "And I can't do that if I'm partying all the time. I've still got so much I need to work on."

"You're a good player, Jadon, but you're not going to play for England, none of us are," one of his team-mates replied. "We'll be lucky if we even play for City."

Jadon didn't reply. He didn't need to be told by anybody about how good he was (or wasn't).

He knew he was going to play for England, and that was that.

7
PEPPED

October 2016, Manchester City training ground
Manchester, England

When Jadon first read the text on his phone, his mind started racing. He'd done it.

Then he checked the back of the phone, just to make sure that it was his, and he hadn't picked up someone else's phone by mistake.

It *was* his phone, and the message most definitely *was* for him.

He had been invited to train with the first team at City.

Jadon jumped up and down, punching the air.

If he was honest, he'd been expecting this, after storming to the U18s title with his fellow Man City youth players, Brahim Díaz, Manu García and Phil Foden.

On top of that, he'd already made his debut for the England U16 team, and he was now really beginning to stand out, even amongst some of the most talented players in the country.

But even so, it still felt incredible to get the City call-up officially.

His first day with the first team squad came around quickly, and Jadon walked out onto the training pitch trying to feel as cool as he hoped he looked.

The whole place was charged with a new kind of energy and Jadon could see the man behind it all waving him over.

Pep Guardiola – the newly appointed City manager.

Jadon walked over to Pep, trying to hide a wide grin.

Here was the man who had coached Lionel Messi, Robert Lewandowski and Thierry Henry, and now Jadon was standing in front of him, ready to listen.

"Jadon," said Pep, shaking his hand energetically and putting his arm around him. "It's good to see you here."

Jadon nodded, unable to get a word out. He didn't need to though, as Pep had plenty more to say.

"I like you, Jadon. You're just what I want in my team. You play fearless football and you don't go for the safe option in games. And that takes confidence, which I like."

He relaxed his grip on Jadon's arm and started gesticulating as he spoke.

"Everyone thinks I only love passing, that I'm all pass, pass, pass," said Pep, "but that's not true. Football should be exciting, don't you think?"

Jadon nodded, again feeling tongue-tied.

"So, you shouldn't be scared to run at people, dribble, shoot, cross," Pep went on. "You have good instincts, Jadon, and when it's one-on-one, I know you'll beat the other man."

Jadon stood there, trying to take it all in. It was hard to follow Pep's rapid stream of thoughts, but out of everything his new manager had said, the same words kept running through his mind, again and again.

Pep had told him, "You're just what I want in my team ... "

His talk with Pep (OK, so Pep had done most of the talking) only increased Jadon's determination that day. He warmed up at a distance from the superstars on the field and took his place for the practice game they were going to play.

But when he saw who was marking him, his mouth dropped open.

"Let's see what you've got then," said Raheem Sterling, narrowing his eyes slightly.

The whistle went for the start of the game and it didn't take Jadon long to realise the huge challenges facing him.

Raheem definitely knew how to mark a player and shut him down.

At one point Jadon actually managed to turn Raheem inside out, and there were jeers and cheers from the players about the sixteen-year-old who'd just nutmegged City's main man.

"What was that about?" Raheem shouted, but there was a smile on his face and Jadon could see that he wasn't annoyed. " 'You trying to embarrass me, Jadon?"

"No way!" Jadon replied. "It was just the best way to get past you."

"Well, you almost did my back in."

They laughed and, after playing the match out, Jadon found himself walking off the pitch with Raheem.

Immediately it was as if they'd known each other for years. They spoke about all the things they had in common – street football in London, moving up north, and their young lives and careers.

"I just want to be playing as much football as possible," Jadon told Raheem. "I want to put the hours in, so I get better and better."

"I was just like that when I was your age," Raheem replied. "There's always another step you can take, always one more thing you can do."

"Yeah," Jadon said. "Nobody else seems to get it."

"I think only the best players have it," Raheem answered, "and it's a good thing. As long as you don't get bored of football and you've got the ability, it's easy to improve. You've just got to get out there and keep practising."

Jadon nodded, feeling a warm glow. Here he was, talking with and playing with someone he genuinely looked up to – and it all felt so normal.

"Or just watch Kevin," Raheem added as he jogged off, pointing to Kevin De Bruyne. A second later De Bruyne whipped in a brilliant cross for Sergio Agüero to tap into the back of the net.

Jadon had just seen what the level was. Now, he just needed to match it.

8
FRIEND AND FOE

March 2017, Emirates Stadium, London, England
Arsenal U23 v Man City U23

As Jadon pulled up his socks and headed out onto the pitch, he couldn't hide his feelings of disappointment. He wasn't playing for the first team.

Weeks had turned into months and still Jadon's name hadn't appeared on City's team sheet.

Yes, he'd got to train with the first team every now and then. Yes, he was praised for being "one of the best players they'd worked with," and, yes, there were throwaway mentions of "when his debut comes".

But there seemed to be nothing behind any of these words. There'd been no actual debut and there was no timeline for when that might change.

Jadon felt stuck in the U23s.

Today the City U23s were away to Arsenal, and there would be a face on the pitch that he hadn't seen for a while.

"Ready to lose?" Reiss Nelson asked with a smile, as they shook hands at the start of the game.

Jadon grinned. For all his frustrations, life was good. He was back in London, he was seeing his friend and he was about to play one of the best U23 sides in the country.

The likes of Carl Jenkinson and Yaya Sanogo were starting for Arsenal, and they were joined by Ainsley Maitland-Niles and Eddie Nketiah. No doubt about it – it was a very good team.

Jadon felt a sudden burst of energy.

Today was as good a day as any to show Pep what he was missing.

As they took their places, Jadon spoke to the team-mates around him loudly enough for Reiss to hear.

"Don't worry about Nelson, mate. He's rubbish – just let him have the ball and he'll muck it up all by himself."

Jadon was delighted that, despite Arsenal's experience, City quickly stormed into a 2-0 lead, thanks to a brace from young striker Thierry Ambrose.

Although they were on opposite ends of the pitch, and so didn't have many opportunities to interact, Jadon managed to drop deep at one point and flick the ball around Reiss, which gave him a rush.

Despite City's lead, Arsenal managed to get back into it, with a couple of quick goals either side of half-time. Reiss was heavily involved in both of them, setting up Donyell Malen for the first one, before firing in a strike of his own in the second half.

"Your turn now, Jadon," Reiss said, as he jogged back to the half-way line.

It felt almost as if they were back on the playground

in South London, each of them trying to outdo the other.

When Lukas Nmecha fired City into the lead from the penalty spot, it looked for a moment as if they were going to take all three points back to Manchester.

Jadon was feeling sure that, this time, he would have the bragging rights over his old mate.

But there were five minutes of extra time and Arsenal were busy piling on the pressure. They just had too many quality players and eventually Eddie Nketiah was able to poke the ball to Carl Jenkinson, who finished it off.

The final score was 3-3, and both teams had played out an incredible game for the small number of fans who had turned up to watch.

At full time Reiss came straight up to Jadon and they swapped shirts. Back in the cages in South London, they'd promised each other that they'd do this when they got to the big leagues.

"But we're not quite in the big leagues yet," Jadon muttered.

The game had pushed all the feelings of disappointment out of his mind but, now that the match was over, they all flooded back. Jadon had a sense of urgency, of wanting to achieve.

"It'll come," Reiss said, as they wandered off the pitch together. "Look at Mbappé, right? He's 17 and he's tearing it up for Monaco this season. Our clubs will be on it, they'll see the ability we've got. Age doesn't matter."

"I'm just worried that, for every match I'm not getting game time, my football is suffering," Jadon replied.

"Relax, man." Reiss tried to soothe his friend. "You've got the assurances from the club and from Pep. You're on his radar. You just have to be patient."

But a voice in the back of Jadon's head told him otherwise.

For now, he put it out of his mind. But he knew that waiting around was not his style.

9
PLAYING THE GAME

July 2017, Manchester City training ground
Manchester, England

"Pep's ready for you," said the coaching assistant, waving Jadon and his agent towards the manager's office.

Jadon smiled. He was certainly ready for what Pep had to say.

Looking back at the last season, in the UEFA Youth League – the U19 equivalent of the Champions

League – he'd scored twice. He'd also scored twice against the Sunderland and Tottenham U23s and he'd played a key role in the team reaching the FA Youth Cup final.

Then, in the first major international competition of his career, the U17 Euros in May, he'd spent most of every game with the ball at his feet.

In fact, the role he'd played in getting England to the final was so crucial that he'd been chosen as the competition's best player.

To top things off, the City chairman Khaldoon Al Mubarak had spoken publicly in glowing terms about Jadon, Phil and Brahim, and Pep had already declared that the three of them were going to be first-team players.

So, surely, it was a no-brainer?

Jadon knew that this meeting with Pep would be about his new contract, his debut and his role in the team.

"Jadon!" the City chairman grinned as soon as Jadon walked in, extending his hand in greeting. Jadon took it. He was glad to be here and he felt confident.

"I'm sure you know why you're here, Jadon. We want to talk about a new contract, make sure you're with us for the long term. How does that sound?"

"Yeah, that sounds good," said Jadon, flicking a glance towards Pep Guardiola, whose expression was difficult to read.

"So I'm going to lay out the terms here," Khaldoon continued, presenting a few sheets of paper which had all the financials of the contract laid out on them.

Jadon passed it all over to his agent.

Jadon wasn't too bothered by the money, though he could see from the look on his agent's face that it was a significant increase on his current deal.

Jadon just wanted to talk about playing time. He didn't want to sit on big money in the reserves – he wanted to be playing in the squad.

"And what would my role be?" he asked.

Pep and the chairman exchanged glances.

"Well that's something we'd have to discuss," said Khaldoon, leading the conversation.

"Aren't we going to discuss it now?" said Jadon, sitting a little straighter in his chair. Surely all the praise lavished on him had just been leading up to this moment?

"Sign the contract first, Jadon. Then we can talk about how we plan to use you," said Pep, speaking up for the first time.

Jadon looked at the two men. This didn't sound right to him.

"I want an assurance – in writing – that I'll get at least 15 games in all competitions in the next season," he said, trying to sound more confident than he felt on the inside.

Before the meeting, Jadon had discussed with his agent how he was going to ask for more playing time. Now Jadon wanted to make sure that he said it exactly right.

Once more, Pep Guardiola and Khaldoon Al Mubarak looked at each other. Something was going on that Jadon didn't feel good about.

"I don't know if we can do that, Jadon," Pep said slowly. "But you're one of the best young players we've seen, and I know you'll be incredible when your debut comes. When the time is right."

A thought occurred to Jadon before Pep had even finished speaking. He was not going to be in this team. He felt sure about it, and he knew that if he thought otherwise he'd be deluding himself.

Pep had done this before – making him think he was going to be in the team.

But it hadn't happened then, and it wasn't happening now. He'd led Jadon on, and he was just going to keep on doing it, again and again.

Jadon felt an uncomfortable sinking feeling, quickly followed by a spark of defiance.

Since he'd been a child Jadon had always been able to see a situation for what it was. Here was a manager doing the right thing for the team, buying experienced forwards, collecting them, but ultimately keeping players like Jadon on the sidelines.

This was not what Jadon wanted.

Even after his debut, it wouldn't be guaranteed that he'd be chosen regularly over the likes of Raheem and other players.

He was being taught to be selfless, to be a team player, but years of street football had told him that sometimes in this game it had to be every man for himself.

Jadon looked Pep straight in the eye. He was sitting in front of perhaps the best manager in the world, but that didn't matter to Jadon. What mattered to him was playing football.

"I think I'm going to leave it, then," he said.

As Jadon spoke, adrenaline surged through his body, but he focused on keeping his expression calm and polite.

He wasn't exactly sure what was said after that, as he sat through the rest of the meeting in a kind of daze.

All he knew was that he wouldn't change his mind. His dad had raised him to be confident in his decisions and he was sure that, here, he was doing the right thing.

When Jadon finally walked out of the office, he ran straight into Raheem Sterling in the corridor outside.

"How'd it go?" Raheem asked cheerfully, oblivious to the situation.

"They wouldn't offer me solid playing time, so I told them I couldn't sign the contract. I'm leaving."

Raheem's eyes widened, his face accidentally betraying what he must have been thinking: *This boy is crazy.*

It was a look that Jadon knew he was going to have to get used to. From now on, he would be the 17-year-old boy who'd walked away from Pep Guardiola.

"I can't say I was expecting that, Jadon," Raheem said finally.

Jadon shrugged. "It's the right thing for me," he said.

The atmosphere at the Man City ground over the next few weeks was tough, but Jadon remained single-minded about his decision.

Stories of players at big clubs who were left on the sidelines and who, over time, amounted to nothing were common, and Jadon would not, *could* not, let himself be another one of them.

News of Jadon's refusal to sign soon got out and the

press were incensed by the story. How could such a young kid be so arrogant? And Man City, of all clubs!

When Jadon had told Reiss, his friend had thought that he was joking at first, but he knew Jadon and he knew how sure he was about what he should do.

His dad was the only person who didn't seem at all surprised, and when Jadon started missing training sessions, he was the only one who really understood why.

When Jadon was left out of Man City's pre-season tour of the USA, he wasn't bothered. He knew he had talent and he knew that soon other clubs would come calling.

He just hoped that they saw the way to his heart. Not with new football boots or praise, but with guaranteed minutes on the pitch, playing the game he loved.

10
A NEW PATH

August 2017, Dortmund, North Rhine-Westphalia, Germany

Jadon had been right. Other clubs *were* interested in him, and the call from his agent came sooner than he'd expected.

"Someone's interested, Jadon – someone I think you'll like the sound of."

Jason pressed the phone closer to his ear. "Go on," he said.

"It's abroad, in Germany, but it's a team known for playing its younger players. Borussia Dortmund."

His agent paused to let it sink in, then added, "So what do you think?"

Jadon's mind started spinning. The German Bundesliga was one of the greatest leagues in the world, and Dortmund's stadium was the biggest in Germany.

He tried to focus his thoughts as he thought about such a move. It would be a very different path from the one he thought he'd be taking.

But even before the phone call had ended, Jadon knew it just felt right.

He was confident. He knew he could do this, especially after the moves to Watford and to City, both of which had got him used to change.

He just needed to know that the German club could offer him the one thing Man City wouldn't – game time.

It wasn't long before he met with Borussia Dortmund manager Peter Bosz and their Director of Football,

Michael Zorc. They'd recently sold their star winger Ousmane Dembélé to Barcelona for well over 100 million euros and they were looking to spend that money on their squad.

"I'm so glad we could sit down with you, Jadon," Zorc said, his face beaming. "When we heard that you were leaving Man City, we couldn't believe it!"

"Yeah, you and the rest of the world," said Jadon with a grin.

"We've been following you for quite some time," Zorc continued, "and we really want you here. We're experts at buying underused and emerging players and turning them into superstars."

Zorc paused before carrying on with his pitch. "We want to give you the number 7 shirt. You're going to be a big part of our first team this year, Jadon. Ain't that right, Peter?"

Peter Bosz nodded, which was a reassuring sign for Jadon.

"Yeah, that sounds great!" Jadon replied, breathing deeply and trying not to be swept away by it all. It was beginning to look like a dream move for him.

But there was one thing he needed to know for sure before he made his decision.

"If I join you," Jadon continued, "I won't let you down. But I need some real guarantees about game time."

"You have our personal assurance," the manager said firmly. "You'll be playing. Don't doubt that for a second."

"But," Zorc went on, "we do need one assurance from you. You know that the U17 World Cup is in October, in India, and we're pretty sure that you'll be part of the England squad for it."

He paused, before carrying on. "We'd prefer that you didn't go to India for it at all, but we understand that you'll want to. So, as a compromise, we'd like to suggest that you go, but that you go only for the group stages, so your training here isn't too disrupted."

Jadon thought for a moment. The World Cup was huge, and he'd already imagined himself playing in all the England games, getting through to the final and holding the Cup high as England won the tournament.

But he could see where Dortmund were coming from.

Being there for just the group stages would be a sacrifice, but that kind of thing hadn't stopped him before.

"OK," he said after a long pause, letting a grin spread over his face. "It's a deal. I'll do it."

By the end of August, Jadon was a Dortmund player. It was a relatively small fee of about £8 million, but for a player who was yet to play a senior game and was just 17 years old, it was huge.

He just prayed that he'd be able to make it worth their while.

11
CHILE IN THE HEAT

October 2017, Kolkata, India

As Jadon sat in the dressing room and pulled on his England shirt before the game, he thought about how crazy the last few months had been.

He was now a few months into his Dortmund career and, if he was honest, it had all been a lot harder than he'd expected.

A few doubts about whether he'd done the right

thing had even started to creep into the back of his mind.

Jadon was yet to make his first-team debut for Dortmund, and he'd been spending a lot of time training rather than actually playing.

On top of that, he didn't have any friends his own age in Germany, plus he was struggling a bit with the language. He'd ended up hanging out a lot with Christian Pulisic, the young American winger who was a regular in the team.

Jadon had also been getting some unofficial coaching from Marco Reus, the experienced German winger.

"You want to wrap your foot around it, Jadon," he said, demonstrating it himself. "Do it like this and aim it right into that far corner."

"I know how to do that, man," Jadon laughed. "The only thing I need you to help me with is my German, not football!"

"You've got a lot of confidence, I'll give you that," Reus said, shaking his head. "Come back to me when you've realised you've got some more to learn."

Today's game was England's first in the U17 World Cup. It was against Chile, in the stifling Indian heat.

The England squad was pretty much the same as the one that had reached the final of the European Championships. England had some of the best young players in Europe and were one of the pre-tournament favourites.

Looking around the dressing room, Jadon could see his old Man City teammates Phil Foden and Joel Latibeaudiere, as well as familiar faces such as Angel Gomes, Callum Hudson-Odoi and Rhian Brewster.

Within five minutes of kick-off, England struck. Jadon picked up the ball just inside the Chile half and began running at the defenders.

He could see them panicking as he moved forward and skipped past them. Glancing over, he spotted Hudson-Odoi making a run across goal. He slipped the ball into him and let his teammate do the rest.

England had the first goal.

The rest of the first half was tight and England struggled to break down the resolute Chile defence. Jadon saw a couple of chances flash wide.

"We need that second goal, lads," he said, trying to fire the players up as they came out for the second half. They all knew that the longer it stayed at 1-0, the more confident Chile would become.

Ten minutes later, England doubled their lead.

Rhian Brewster spun away down the right and his cross found the Chilean keeper, but the keeper's weak parry landed at Jadon's feet.

Jadon didn't need a second invitation to tuck the ball away.

2-0.

"That's got to be the win now," he panted to Phil Foden.

Jadon's second came moments later.

George McEachran slipped the ball to him and, finding himself with tons of space, Jadon whipped it into the far corner of the goal, the way that Reus had been trying to teach him to do at Dortmund.

"I told him I already knew how to do it," Jadon

muttered happily to himself, as they restarted the game.

A stunning free kick from England captain Angel Gomes sealed the win for England, as they began the tournament with a thumping 4-0 victory.

"Let's keep this going, boys!" Gomes shouted, as they walked off down the tunnel at the end of the game.

They did keep it going over the next two group games, with a narrow 3-2 win over Mexico followed by a 4-0 thrashing of Iraq.

This was the end of the group games, so it was the point when Jadon had to return to Germany – to go back to Dortmund, just as he'd promised Michael Zorc when he'd joined the club.

Jadon half-wished now that he could stay on in India with England. He was sure he could help them go on and win it – but he'd made a commitment to Dortmund and he knew he had to honour it.

"Sorry lads," he said, addressing the whole team after the Iraq game. "I wish I could stick with you, but I know you can do this. I'll be watching every game, so you'd better bring that trophy home!"

He was met by cheers from the players, despite their disappointment at his leaving.

On the flight back to Germany, Jadon thought long and hard about his immediate future. He was going back to Dortmund – to *his* club.

They had put their faith in him, and now it was his turn to deliver. He decided that, whatever happened, he was going to make it work.

When the plane touched down in Germany, he felt a new level of determination.

12
DEBUT

October 2017, Waldstadion, Frankfurt, Germany
Borussia Dortmund v Eintracht Frankfurt

Jadon's determination was quickly vindicated and, just a week later, he was included in the Borussia Dortmund squad for the first time. It was for an away game at Eintracht Frankfurt.

Jadon started on the bench, alongside the likes of Shinji Kagawa and Andriy Yarmolenko, and he didn't really expect to get any time on the pitch.

At half-time Dortmund were leading comfortably and Jadon's hopes were raised. With such a strong lead, perhaps the manager wouldn't mind giving him some minutes.

But Jadon's hopes were dashed as Frankfurt pulled themselves back into the game, making it 2-2 with over 20 minutes remaining.

Now, Jadon knew, Dortmund needed to turn to their big guns. It would be Yarmolenko or maybe Jacob Bruun Larsen who would be called on, not him.

But, with five minutes remaining, Peter Bosz looked over at the bench.

"Jadon!" he shouted, making himself heard over the din of the crowd. "Come on, get up! You're on."

Jadon couldn't believe his ears. The two words "You're on" echoed around his head as he went through the motions of adjusting his shin pads.

He felt like he'd been playing for years, but he suddenly realised that he'd never actually made a senior professional appearance.

This was going to be his debut.

He'd been dreaming of this day ever since he was a

little boy, but he'd never thought it would come in Germany, let alone for Borussia Dortmund.

But here he was.

Jadon jogged up to his manager, wondering what last-minute instructions he was going to get.

"Just go out there and do what you do best," said Bosz. "Panic them, run at them, embarrass them. Trust your instincts."

Jadon just nodded. He had no words to say.

"Prove to everyone that you deserve that number 7 shirt," Bosz growled, before slapping him on the back and giving him a shove out onto the turf.

Jadon's time on the pitch seemed to pass in seconds. He barely touched the ball, and whenever he did he found himself having to make a quick pass, instead of keeping possession.

It was frustrating and exhilarating, all at the same time.

Jadon made no impact on the game and it finished at 2-2.

But it didn't matter. He'd made his debut.

As he walked off the pitch alongside Mario Götze

and Pierre-Emerick Aubameyang, Jadon knew that he'd been right to stick with Dortmund.

Not for the first time in his career, he'd made the right decision.

13
BACK IN THE GAME

April 2018, Signal Iduna Park, Dortmund, Germany
Borussia Dortmund v Bayer Leverkusen

Jadon's debut hadn't led to the run of games he'd hoped for. A ligament injury early on had curtailed the start to his Dortmund career.

He'd watched on the TV back at home as his team-mates for the England under 17s had lifted the World Cup.

They'd overcome a dramatic penalty shootout

against Japan and had then come back from 2-0 down against Spain in the final to win it.

Jadon's medal had been given to him separately, and part of him still wished that he'd turned down Dortmund, so that he could have been there on the pitch, holding the cup aloft with the rest of the England squad.

Watching the win on TV only strengthened his desire to make his debut for the senior England team one day. Maybe he could be the one finally to help them win a major trophy.

While he was recovering from his injury, he'd also been forced to watch on TV as Dortmund had been dumped out of both Europe and the German Cup.

They were well behind Bayern in the title race too, and star striker Pierre-Emerick Aubameyang had departed for Arsenal.

All-round it was turning into a bad season for the club, and manager Peter Bosz had been sacked in mid-December. He'd been replaced by another Peter, in the form of Peter Stöger.

When Jadon returned from his injury layoff, it was

Peter Stöger who handed him a place back in the first-team squad and allowed him to play a few games from the bench.

"How are you doing after the injury?" Marco Reus asked Jadon, on his first training session back with the squad.

"Yeah, I think I'm doing alright," Jadon replied, stretching his legs and feeling for any pain or tightness.

"It's not easy to come back from a bad injury like that," Reus continued. "I've had a few myself. Trust me, I know what I'm talking about."

Jadon nodded. Anyone who'd watched any football over the last few years would be familiar with Marco Reus' injury record.

"Just don't overdo it when you first come back," said Reus. "I know the temptation is to dive into that first training session – you know, prove yourself – but that'll only make it worse. Yeah? You have to take it slow."

Reus had a doubtful look on his face, as if he didn't

believe Jadon could take anything to do with football slowly.

In fact, Reus' advice went against everything Jadon stood for.

Jadon believed that hard work and dedication were the best ways to improve and to learn. If he worked harder than everyone else, he'd do better and he'd end up being selected above them.

Nevertheless, he took on board what Reus had said and tried to ease himself gradually back into his football.

It seemed to work, and by the beginning of April he couldn't feel any issues in the leg that had troubled him.

If anything, he felt sharper, quicker, and he was ready to get back out on the pitch again.

Jadon was handed his first start after his return from injury in April's big game against Bayer Leverkusen.

Needing a win, Peter Stöger had decided that Dortmund were going to attack the game, so he'd started pretty much every attacking player in the squad.

It paid off when, within 15 minutes, Dortmund got their first breakthrough.

Christian Pulisic darted in from the right-hand side and slid the ball over to Jadon.

The Leverkusen defender had slipped, giving Jadon a chance. Jadon opened up his body and tucked the ball into the far corner of the goal.

GOAL!

There it was. His first professional goal.

It had come much earlier in his career than he'd anticipated, and he felt that weight lifted from his shoulders. Some players went years before getting their first.

Jadon sprinted over to the corner flag, grabbing his shirt but otherwise not really sure how to celebrate. He jumped into the air, reaching up and punching the sky as he did so.

Marco Reus came jogging up behind him.

"Yeah, I guess you don't really need to learn that finish, do you?" he laughed.

"I might need to teach it to you!" Jadon joked. "It's your turn to get a goal now."

For the next 40 minutes it looked as if Jadon's goal was going to be the only difference between the sides.

That was until Dortmund's Max Phillip slipped the ball in for Marco Reus, who rounded the goalkeeper and finished with ease.

Dortmund were now in control. They had the safety net of a second goal and could start to enjoy their football and play with a bit more freedom.

Ten minutes later, the game was done and dusted. Jadon controlled a long ball forward with the back of his heel, bringing it down into his path.

He skipped his way forward past a defender, then flicked the ball back to Max Phillip, who controlled it then stabbed it past the goalkeeper.

Jadon had already turned to celebrate as Phillip chased after him.

"That touch was amazing, Jadon!" Phillip said, pointing to where Jadon had brought the ball down. "How did you do that?"

"I don't know. It was instinct, I didn't think about it,"

Jadon replied, a big grin on his face. "I'm glad I could help you score, though."

With 10 minutes of the game remaining, Jadon was once more at the centre of things. He picked the ball up on the left-hand side, spotting Marco Reus lurking at the back post.

Jadon floated a cross into the box, which landed perfectly on the head of Reus, who directed the ball back into the goal.

"You need to set me up next!" Jadon shouted, as they walked back to the half-way line, ready for the game to kick off again.

It was the last of the goals, but it didn't matter. It was a thumping 4-0 victory over one of the biggest teams in Germany.

And with a goal and two assists under his belt, Jadon was named Man of the Match. It was easy to see why.

By now Jadon was even starting to make headlines back in England, and there were some rumours that he was going to get a late call-up to the England World Cup squad.

Jadon couldn't quite believe them. He'd only just started playing for the England U19s with Reiss Nelson. Surely there was no way he could make it to the main England squad as well.

The rumours proved to be unfounded and Jadon didn't get the call from Gareth Southgate.

Instead, he remained with Borussia Dortmund and trained under their new manager, Lucien Favre.

He was the third manager Dortmund had had in Jadon's short time there, and Jadon wasn't quite sure how he fitted in with the new manager's approach to the game.

Nevertheless, he was confident that he could win a place in the side, even if the manager turned out not to be a fan. Jadon had always risen to the occasion, wherever he'd played.

Jadon also made sure he'd watched the England senior team as they achieved their best performance at a World Cup for over 20 years, losing to Belgium in the third-place play-offs.

"I want to be in this team, man," he muttered to Reiss Nelson as they watched the Belgium game on the TV.

"They might have won it if they'd had you there," Reiss replied jokingly.

"Maybe." Jadon laughed, but he wasn't joking.

He was sure that if he'd been there, he would have made a difference.

14
ON THE BENCH

October 2018, Signal Iduna Park, Dortmund, Germany
Borussia Dortmund v RB Leipzig

The arrival of new manager Lucien Favre wasn't the only thing that had changed for Jadon's second season in Germany. Dortmund had also signed some big-name players in Axel Witsel, Paco Alcácer and Achraf Hakimi.

Jadon had also been joined in Germany by Reiss Nelson.

Reiss hadn't joined Dortmund, but he'd gone on loan from Arsenal to Hoffenheim.

For Jadon, it was good to have an old friend around, even if they rarely had the opportunity to hang out together, both being so busy with their clubs.

"I can't believe you've come out here," Jadon laughed, as they met up on Reiss's first day in Germany. "You need to get your own ideas and stop copying me!"

"Hey man, it wasn't my idea," Reiss replied, raising his hands in the air. "Arsenal forced me to do it. *I* wanted to go somewhere decent."

"Sure you did," said Jadon, shaking his head.

"So, what are Hoffenheim like anyway?" Reiss asked. "Are they any good?"

Jadon frowned. "Didn't you do any research? How can you not know anything about the team you're going to play for?"

"I don't have time for that kind of stuff," said Reiss, trying to be serious. "I'm too busy playing football."

"They're pretty good," said Jadon. "They've got this top young manager. They could be pushing for Europe this season, but they're normally mid-table."

"Oh, right," Reiss said, nodding along.

"So, not that different to Arsenal!" Jadon added cheekily.

Reiss threw him a look.

The start of the season rolled around quickly. Dortmund began their campaign with a big game against RB Leipzig.

Jadon found himself starting on the bench, with Lucien Favre preferring Marco Reus and Christian Pulisic in attack.

Both forwards had good games and Jadon didn't get on until the final 10 minutes of the match.

Even though he was only on the pitch for such a short time, he was still able to get an assist for Marco Reus.

"I'm glad you came on," Reus said, wrapping his arm around Jadon's shoulders as they walked off at full time. "I needed someone to set me up."

"Thanks, man," Jadon sighed. "I wish I could have played a bit longer though – or, you know, maybe even started."

"Don't worry," said Reus. "It'll come."

Over the next few weeks the games continued in the same frustrating pattern for Jadon.

Dortmund were winning the games, but he was being limited to a substitute's role. He would come on for the last 10 or 15 minutes of a game, and often even then he would only get an assist.

But he wasn't getting any starts, and what he *was* achieving obviously wasn't enough to change the manager's mind.

"What do I need to do?" he would moan to anyone who would listen.

"To be fair, Jadon, Christian and Marco are in great form," Axel Witsel pointed out one day in the dressing room. "Your best hope is probably that one of them gets injured."

"It's just my luck that the one season Marco Reus is fully fit is the one season that I want to get in the side," Jadon said, trying to laugh at his own misfortune.

However, it did seem that he hadn't lost his form. By

the beginning of October he'd got five assists in the league, despite the fact he was yet to start a game.

Axel was right. He needed to hang on in there. Things were bound to change.

15
"IT'S GARETH"

October 2018, Stadion Rujevica, Rijeka, Croatia
Croatia v England

Jadon had slumped down on the sofa, feeling tired after an intense training session. Whenever he wasn't getting time on the pitch, training always felt harder, but Jadon knew he had to persevere. It mattered.

This time his thoughts had been interrupted by the ringing of his mobile phone.

He'd expected it to be Reiss or his dad, but at first

he didn't recognise the voice on the other end of the phone.

"Jadon? It's Gareth. Can we talk?"

Gareth. Gareth Southgate.

Jadon had managed to keep his cool during the conversation, but as soon as he'd hung up he'd jumped and punched the air. It had been the news he'd been dreaming of since he'd been a little kid.

He was going to be in the England squad.

His first England game was away to Croatia, the team that had knocked England out of the World Cup just three months earlier.

Jadon started on the bench, watching some of the biggest names in the country take to the pitch.

There was an eerie quiet to the stadium, as the match was being played behind closed doors (a punishment for the Croatians, as a result of crowd trouble in a previous game). It was a real contrast to the wall of noise that Jadon was used to at Dortmund and took some getting used to.

The game played out without any goals, and with just 10 minutes of the game left, and the score still stuck at 0-0, Jadon was called over by Southgate.

"You're on, Jadon. Go and play your natural game," he said. "Go and see if you can get a goal."

Jadon was replacing his old friend Raheem Sterling.

"I knew you'd be playing for England one day, bro," Raheem smiled as they swapped over on the touchline. "I didn't think it would be so soon, though."

Jadon ran onto the pitch determined to make his mark, but although he had a couple of chances he couldn't make an impact and the game ran out 0-0.

It wasn't the debut Jadon had wanted, but it didn't matter.

Whatever happened between now and the end of his career, he'd always have this simple fact to remember: he'd been an England international.

16
A STARTER FOR TWO

October 2018, Signal Iduna Park, Dortmund, Germany
Borussia Dortmund v Hertha Berlin

Jadon returned to Dortmund with renewed confidence. He knew the England bosses were watching him now and he wanted to impress. His England appearances had put him on the world stage, and now there were a lot of clubs from around Europe who had their eyes on him.

Dortmund were desperate to keep him, but they knew that to do that, they had to play him.

Jadon had been gradually getting more game time at the club, and then, for todays's game against Hertha Berlin, he was named in the starting eleven.

This was a big game. Dortmund had made a good start to the season, but if they wanted to wrestle the title from Bayern, they needed to win today.

Jadon had a goal disallowed after just 20 minutes, but he could feel he was starting to find his rhythm. He was going to score today – he just knew it.

A few minutes later, Dortmund burst forward with Mario Götze leading the charge. Driving deep into the Hertha half, Götze flicked the ball past the defence, straight into Jadon's path.

The keeper had already committed and Jadon needed to do little more than tuck it into the unguarded net.

"That one will count!" he roared as he celebrated the goal.

But Dortmund's lead didn't last long, as Salomon Kalou poked Hertha Berlin back on level terms just before half-time.

Then, 15 minutes into the second half, Jadon

responded in turn. Achraf Hakimi played the ball into the box and, when Reus missed it, Jadon was there, standing on the line to tap it in.

"That's probably one of your best goals, Jadon!" Reus joked. Reus was right – it wasn't one of his best. But they all counted.

It wasn't quite enough though, as Salomon Kalou struck once more before the end of the match to make it 2-2.

Dortmund hadn't quite done enough to win the game, but Jadon had been impressive – and he knew it. He'd now scored four times in his last three games.

"If this doesn't get me in the side, I don't know what will," he said to Axel Witsel as they left the pitch.

Back in the dressing room after the game, Jadon noticed Reus looking at him thoughtfully.

"You know, Jadon, when you first came here, I don't think you ever really passed the ball," said Reus.

"What do you mean?" Jadon asked. He thought he'd always been pretty selfless.

"You used to do all these skills," said Reus, "but then you'd cross it way too hard or you'd have a shot. I thought you were going to be this cocky little kid who would always shoot first."

"But you tried to teach me shooting!" Jadon replied. "I was probably following your advice!"

"I only tried to teach you shooting because I thought, well, if you're going to shoot you might as well do it properly," Reus laughed.

"I told you I already knew how to shoot well," Jadon protested.

"Yeah that's the problem," said Reus. "Every time I go to teach you something, I notice that you're already doing it in training, or you're do it in a match. And now you're a really good passer and a good crosser too!"

"And you've had nothing to do with it!" Jadon interjected. He meant this as a joke, but Reus gave him a long look.

"Careful," said Reus. "I'm still your captain, mate."

17
DOUBTS

April 2019, Signal Iduna Park, Dortmund, Germany
Borussia Dortmund v Mainz

Jadon had been right to be confident that he would win his place in the side. He soon became a regular starter for Borussia Dortmund, replacing his friend Christian Pulisic in the first eleven.

Jadon had already got more assists than anyone else in the league, and he still hadn't even turned nineteen.

If Christian Pulisic was disappointed to have lost his

place in the side, then Marco Reus and Paco Alcácer were absolutely delighted to see Jadon playing.

They were benefitting from Jadon's generosity with the ball, and they were scoring goal after goal as Dortmund shot to the top of the Bundesliga.

Even so, the last few months had been a rollercoaster ride for Jadon and for the club.

In the Champions League Dortmund had started strongly, with Jadon making his Champions League debut and getting his first Champions League goal in a 4-0 win against Atlético Madrid.

That had been a real statement of intent from Dortmund, soundly thrashing one of Europe's biggest teams.

Then in the last 16 they'd been drawn against Spurs, and Jadon had made the journey back to England – to London, his home city, for the first leg.

"What can you tell us about Spurs, Jadon?" Paco Alcácer had asked him. "How do they play? What are their weaknesses? How do we beat them?"

"I don't know," Jadon had laughed. "I've never played them!"

"Yeah, but you've played with some of the English players," Alcácer had continued. "Like Harry Kane. How do we stop him?"

"I don't know. Maybe hope he's injured, or has a bad day or something."

As it turned out Kane *had* been injured for the first leg, but it had made little difference, as Dortmund had been soundly beaten 3-0 in front of a large crowd at Wembley.

To make things worse, Jadon had been marked out of the game by Spurs defender Jan Vertonghen at left-back.

That had been a wake-up call for Jadon. It was the first time in his fledgling career that things had gone against him.

He'd had pretty much everything go his way up until then. He'd always had confidence in his football skills, in his commitment to the game and in his ability to make the right decisions.

But suddenly he started to have real doubts about his abilities. Looking back, it hadn't been a good feeling and Jadon hadn't known how to deal with it.

"What if I'm not as good as I think I am?" he asked Reus one day in training, as they prepared for the second leg against Spurs. "I mean, I haven't really done it against any of the big teams."

"Don't be daft, Jadon," Reus replied firmly. "First of all, you probably *aren't* as good as you think you are – I mean, you're 18, so obviously you think you're better than you are."

"Right," Jadon replied hesitantly. He wasn't sure where Reus was going with this.

"But that's a good thing," Reus added. "It's that confidence you've got that meant you could come to Germany and play for us."

"I guess."

"Plus, you're only 18, Jadon!" Reus added. "You're not even *close* to reaching your best. If you were dominating the big games now, then there wouldn't be anywhere else for you to go."

Reus paused, to let it sink in. "But you're not dominating the big games," he continued, "and that means there's still stuff you can learn. There's still room to improve. That's a good thing!"

Jadon nodded. What Reus was saying made a lot of sense.

"You've just got to work out what you struggled with against Vertonghen," Reus continued. "Work out what he did that stopped you. Then you'll know what to do next time, so it doesn't happen again."

It was good advice – just the talk Jadon needed. He'd been close to getting caught up in his own self-doubt.

But he didn't need to be so worried. Reus was right, his career was still very fresh and new, there was still so much more for him to do.

As it turned out, Dortmund lost the second leg of their Champions League fixture with Spurs as well, going out 4-0 on aggregate. Crashing out so heavily had left Dortmund feeling pretty bruised.

They'd also been knocked out of the German Cup, so there was only the league left for them to win.

The goal machine of Jadon, Reus and Alcácer up front had put Dortmund at the top of the league, but Bayern had been right on their heels.

The Dortmund players knew that Bayern were experienced title winners. One slip-up would be enough to let Bayern in and take the title.

The next match had in fact been away to Bayern and both clubs knew exactly how important it was.

Jadon had played the full ninety minutes, but Dortmund's biggest game of the season actually turned into their biggest nightmare. They'd been humiliated 5-0, with Lewandowski scoring twice.

As a result Bayern were now back on top, with all the momentum going their way.

Dortmund were second, but were facing a huge struggle to overturn it and get back on top.

"We need to make sure this game goes our way, lads," Reus said, gathering the team round. "You all know how important it is."

Today's game was against Mainz, and Dortmund badly needed the win to bounce back. If they lost this game then Bayern might well move out of reach at the top.

But given Dortmund's current level of confidence, a win was far easier said than done.

"Come on, lads," Jadon said, trying to get the rest of the squad going. Usually before a match he just focused on his own game but, looking around the dressing room, he could see that the rest of the team were in a low mood.

They needed to believe that they could do this.

Jadon's thoughts went back to that bus full of kids, back in his Watford days. It seemed like another lifetime now, but he'd been the one to turn the mood around then.

He could do it again.

"We can still get the title," he said to the squad. "We just have to win today to stay in there!"

The game started quickly and Jadon led by example, sweeping a Mario Götze cross into the back of the net early on.

It was an emotional goal and a big moment for the club, one that Dortmund badly needed.

"Come on!" Jadon roared. "We can do this!"

Seven minutes later, Jadon struck again. This time it was Thomas Delaney bursting down the left-hand side who set him up, cutting the ball back for Jadon to tuck it into the goal.

It was Jadon's tenth league goal of the season, a huge achievement for him – in fact, for any player.

Dortmund eventually managed to see the game out, winning 2-1. They were keeping pace with Bayern at the top, which meant that they still had a chance of the title. The win was a huge confidence boost too, after some difficult games.

Jadon was over the moon – for the team, but also for himself. Not only had he scored both of the Dortmund goals, but he was the youngest player ever to score 10 Bundesliga goals in a single season.

This was only his first full season, and yet he'd already achieved more then many players managed in their whole careers.

He'd never anticipated himself being a goalscorer but

he was relishing it. Even if this season ended in disappointment, he knew he would do much, much more next year.

But, for now, he was enjoying the moment.

And now he knew, for sure, that any self-doubts he'd had were well behind him.

18
MAKING IT HAPPEN

September 2019, St Mary's Stadium, Southampton, England
England v Kosovo

The 2018-19 season had ended in disappointment for Dortmund.

They'd missed out on the league title, with Bayern Munich overtaking them and finishing top, two points clear, and they'd failed to win a single trophy.

It had been a double disappointment for Jadon, as he'd also been part of the England squad that had lost the Nations League semi-final to the Netherlands. Missing out with both his club and his country had been tough to deal with.

For Jadon, there was a lot riding on the coming season. Dortmund hadn't won a trophy for a few years, and on top of that the Euros were coming up, and Jadon was desperate to be part of the England Euros squad.

All summer, Jadon had been linked with a move back to England, but he'd wanted to remain at Dortmund. He'd only been at the club for a year, and he was keen to establish himself before considering a big move.

Dortmund had sold Christian Pulisic to Chelsea, so Jadon's position in the starting eleven was now more secure. And they'd brought in Thorgan Hazard, Julian Brandt and Mats Hummels. This year, thought Jadon, they had a squad that could really go toe-to-toe with Bayern and challenge for the title.

But for Jadon today it was all about England. Standing on the pitch in Southampton before the game, he couldn't quite believe what was happening.

He was playing in the front three for England, but what made it surreal was the fact that he was playing alongside legends Harry Kane and Raheem Sterling.

The game was against Kosovo, and even though England were expected to win it, the bottom line was that they *had* to get a win to qualify for the European Championships.

But the game got off to the worst possible start when Valon Berisha fired Kosovo ahead after just 30 seconds.

"Heads up, boys!" Harry Kane roared. He was a huge presence on the pitch and Jadon listened to him with admiration.

It was one of Jadon's other heroes, Raheem Sterling, who headed England level, just seven minutes later.

"The game starts again from now, OK lads?" Kane shouted, encouraging them to keep pushing.

Ten minutes later, England got their second. Harry Kane collected the ball, skipped past a Kosovan defender and fired it between the legs of the keeper. England were ahead.

A couple of moments before half-time, Jadon got in

on the action. He picked up the ball on the right-hand side, dancing his way into the box, before firing it across the face of the goal. The ball hit a defender and landed in the back of the net.

"I'm claiming that one!" Jadon joked with Raheem as they celebrated the goal.

A moment later Jadon got a goal that was definitely his. Raheem squared the ball to him and with his first touch he got it out from under his feet. Then with his second he smashed it into the back of the net.

His first goal for England!

For all the goals Jadon had scored in his career, the sound of the crowd cheering this one felt like nothing he'd ever experienced before. It was a sweet moment.

Jadon got his second England goal just moments later. Raheem burst into the box and fired off a shot, but it was saved by the keeper, who couldn't hold it. The ball trickled along the line and Jadon was able to tap it in.

"You've nicked that from me!" Raheem shouted across the box, delight on his face.

"You should have finished it the first time, mate.

I can't keep clearing up after you!" Jadon replied, laughing.

England were now 5-1 up and the game was theirs. Their relentless march towards qualification for the Euros continued.

"Congratulations on your first goals!" Harry Kane said, walking over to Jadon at full-time.

It was the first time that Jadon had ever really spoken to the England captain and he was a little starstruck.

"Thanks," he replied nervously. "It feels good to be out on the pitch, playing for England."

"I know. It's a feeling you never quite get over," Kane replied. "I hope you're going to be with us at the Euros next summer."

And with that Harry Kane jogged away, leaving his words ringing in Jadon's ears. Harry Kane wanted him to be at the Euros next summer.

Well, Jadon was going to do everything he could to make sure that happened.

But between now and then there was Dortmund, and just maybe the time had come to lift a trophy with them.

He had the feeling he could make that happen too.

19
HAT-TRICK

May 2020, Benteler-Arena, Paderborn, Germany
Paderborn v Borussia Dortmund

It had been a long two months without football. COVID-19 had brought the season to a crushing halt, with games and training all cancelled and every player forced to stay at home.

Jadon had found it miserable, stuck inside his house. The two months away from the game had been the longest he'd ever gone without playing football.

Keepy-uppies in the garden and drills had helped keep him fit, but it wasn't the same.

Now, thankfully, football was returning and matches were taking place, but the fans weren't being allowed into the stadiums to watch the games.

It wasn't the same without fans, but even so it was better than the last two months without football.

Dortmund still had an outside chance of snatching the title from Bayern Munich. They'd started the season well, but after losing to Bayern recently they were now outsiders to win the league.

Today, away to Paderborn, Dortmund needed a win. It was an easy match on paper, but Jadon knew that there was no such thing as an easy match in the Bundesliga.

Jadon hadn't scored since the season had restarted after COVID and he was desperate to get some goals again.

The 2020 Euros had been put back to 2021, and Jadon wanted to make sure that he was at the forefront of Southgate's mind.

Not to mention the fact that Dortmund were still in with the chance of a trophy.

After a goalless first half, Lucien Favre was in a furious mood at half-time.

"You're letting yourselves down, boys," he said, not raising his voice but still making his feelings clear. "There might not be fans out here, but they're all watching this game at home. And right now, you're letting them all down. Now, get yourselves together and go out and win this thing. For the fans!"

In the second half Thorgan Hazard promptly opened the scoring, putting Dortmund one up.

Three minutes later, Jadon got his first goal. It was a simple tap-in, but it was his first since the season had started. On top of that, the goal put Dortmund in a dominant position in the game, 2-0 up.

But 20 minutes later Paderborn pulled a goal back. Dortmund had been on the receiving end of comebacks before and Jadon was determined not to let this happen today.

He collected a pass from Hazard, flicked the ball on to his left foot and drilled it past the keeper.

GOAL!

There it was. Dortmund were 3-1 up and Jadon had put two past the keeper.

Could he get a third?

Dortmund dominated the rest of the game, with Hakimi and Schemelzer adding goals as Dortmund raced into a 5-1 lead.

But although chance after chance came Jadon's way, he couldn't quite put any of them away.

They were into added time now and Jadon knew that his chance of getting a hat-trick was slipping further and further away.

A moment later, he got the ball and raced clear.

He had Hazard to his left and he glanced across, looking at him. Jadon knew the that right option was to slip a pass to Hazard, so that he could seal the win.

But he didn't want to. The game was won and he was on for a hat-trick. He was going to have a shot.

Jadon pulled his right foot back and slipped the ball past the keeper at the near post.

GOAL!

Hat-trick! He'd done it!

It was the first hat-trick of his professional career and Jadon savoured every moment of it. It wasn't quite the same without the fans, but even so nobody could take it away from him.

"I knew you weren't going to pass to me!" Hazard shouted, as the players celebrated.

Jadon just smiled. There was a lot to smile about. Football was finally back and he could feel this Dortmund team finally coming together.

More than that, he was now firmly at the forefront of Southgate's plans for England. It might be another year before the Euros began, but Jadon was determined to be there and to be better than ever.

Back at home that night, Jadon got off the phone to his dad and sat thinking about how far he'd come.

He'd left England, his home country, without ever having played a professional football match. He'd left with the footballing world and the press doubting him and even laughing at his decision to walk away from the great Man City.

But now he knew that every decision he'd made in his career so far had been right. His instincts and his self-belief had got him to where he was now.

His dad had been right, trusting Jadon to choose his own path. Germany had been good to him and he owed Dortmund so much. But if he ever returned to play for an English club, he knew now it would be for a fee close to a hundred million. That was just crazy. He couldn't even let himself think that way.

But, more valuable than any transfer fee, Jadon knew that he'd had earned the respect and admiration of the footballing world.

He imagined himself going back to meet his eight-year-old self, that kid kicking a ball at an imaginary goal in Kennington. He imagined telling that kid what the future would bring.

He knew that kid would smile, shrug and say, "Yeah, OK, that sounds pretty good. As long as I can keep playing football."

HOW MANY HAVE YOU READ?

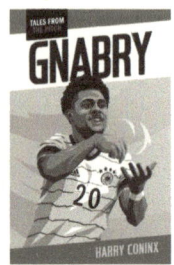

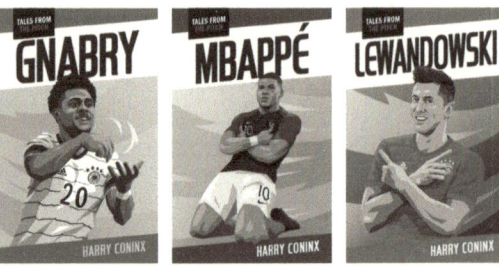

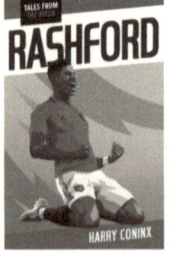

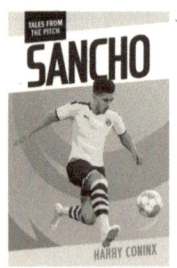

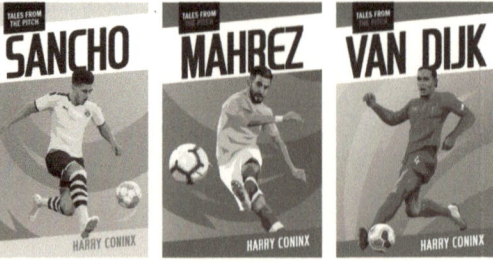

- SILVA
- GNABRY
- MBAPPÉ
- LEWANDOWSKI
- STERLING
- KANTÉ
- RASHFORD
- SON
- FÉLIX
- SANCHO
- MAHREZ
- VAN DIJK